The Miracle Seed

David O. Oyedepo

THE MIRACLE SEED

David O. Oyedepo

Copyright © 1986 by David O. Oyedepo

ISBN 978-2480-00-2

Published in Nigeria by

DOMINION PUBLISHING HOUSE

First published in 1985, reprinted 1986, 1987, 1993, 1995, 2007, 2009, 2010, 2011, 2012

Dominion Publishing House

P.M.B. 21688, Ikeja, Lagos, Nigeria

Tel: 234-1-7747546-8

Web: ww.davidoyedepoministries.org

All Scripture quotations are from the King James Version of the Bible, except otherwise stated.

CONTENTS

INTRODUCTION

There is a craving for the supernatural in all men, regardless of culture and age. Advances in science and technology have not diminished this. The desire for the miraculous seems to be innate, and it accounts for why the magicians and sorcerers on the street attract the crowds they do without publicity. Men, by an instinctive urge, get drawn to such displays.

The only sane explanation for this trait is causally linked with man's original state before the fall. Undoubtedly, the first man, Adam, was a miracle. He lived a miracle-packed life in the Garden of Eden. He was in charge of all the wildest animals one can name. Remember the carnivores we know now, were also carnivores then; the lion did not evolve from a harmless herbivore into a beast of prey, yet it was submissive to Adam. Though Adam fell, man's supernatural characteristics through the finished work of Jesus Christ have been restored in even greater dimensions.

Hence, I believe, the miraculous is still a crowd-puller even in this jet age. The purpose of this book is to show you how to get started on the road to life in the miraculous.

Chapter 1

THE GREATEST MIRACLE

The first man before the fall was a miracle creation. His life was divine; he was king right there in Eden. Everything else God made was under him. He had an extraordinary soundness in his mind. He single-handedly named all the animals, and all of them were obedient to him. Think of the wildest animals today – the lion, the rhino, the leopard, the hippo, etc. – they were all pets in Adam's abode. He was doing with them whatever he pleased. He was really a man to be envied.

Alas, he fell and from being extraordinary, he became ordinary; from being supernatural he became natural. The Bible says in Romans 5:12,

"...By one man sin entered into the world, and death by sin..." This implies that Adam died as soon as he committed the sin of disobedience. He was however, still very much around. Physically he was alive: his muscles and vital parts functioned normally and he did not diminish in size. Nonetheless, the Bible says, he was dead. It was the supernatural element in him that died. We refer to this as the spirit. Man is a triune-nature being: made up of spirit, soul and body. At the fall, man's spirit died, and from then on he lost his supernatural traits. Thank God for a divine remedy, which we now have by Christ Jesus:

> *Wherefore, as by one man sin entered into the world, and death by sin; and so death passed upon all men, for that all have sinned...*
>
> *But not as the offence, so also is the free gift. For if through the offence of one many be dead, much more the grace of*

God, and the gift by grace, which is by one man, Jesus Christ, hath abounded unto many.

Romans 5:12, 15

Thus, what was lost through the first Adam, the second Adam (Jesus Christ) came to restore. The dead spirit can therefore, be brought back to life and this is called the new birth. It is the greatest miracle a man can experience on earth: a rebirth into the realm of the miraculous and the ability to possess the life of God.

Why is this the greatest miracle? Paul the Apostle said in Romans 8:32,

He that spared not his own Son, but delivered him up for us all, how shall he not with him also freely give us all things?

The principal reason Jesus came into the world is to revive again the man God made into the world, not just to heal the sick and

9

perform miracles of various shades, but essentially to bring man back to his rightful place. The miracles were important, but they were not the main reason for His coming and, in particular, for His death on the cross. There were various outstanding miracles way back in the Old Testament times, in the areas of prosperity, deliverance, healing, raising the dead, escaping the horror of the fiery furnace and the jaws of lions, etc. While all these are included in the new covenant, the point still remains that the new birth is the main purpose of Christ's coming. Hebrews 9:22 declares that

> ...*Without shedding of blood is no remission.*

This implies that for man's spirit to be recreated, righteous blood is required to be shed. No wonder, Jesus said, *"It is finished"* while on the cross (Jn. 19:30). The spiritual spell over mankind was dealt with for all time.

Hence, Jesus performed miracles in His

earthly ministry and the Apostles did same. But the greatest miracle of all is the new birth, procured at a great price. The other miracles cost the performers praying, believing and fasting, but this one miracle cost Jesus His life. When you are prayed for, you may have a miracle. For you to become a miracle yourself, you need to be born again. Hear Jesus talking to Nicodemus in John 3:5-8:

> *Jesus answered, Verily, verily, I say unto thee, Except a man be born of water and of the Spirit, he cannot enter into the Kingdom of God.*

> *That which is born of the flesh is flesh; and that which is born of the Spirit is spirit.*

> *Marvel not that I said unto thee, Ye must be born again.*

> *The wind bloweth where it listeth, and thou hearest the sound thereof, but*

> *canst not tell whence it cometh, and*
> *whither it goeth: so is every one that is*
> *born of the Spirit.*

Verse 8 explains the miraculous in the new birth. The newly born-again man is now seated with Jesus in heavenly places, far above principalities and powers. He belongs to the order of men that can tread upon serpents and over all the powers of the enemy, and nothing shall by any means hurt him. Such a man is nothing short of a miracle.

I wish the fundamental problems of the world were merely intellectual, then all professors of knowledge today would be free. But man's problems are basically spiritual. He does not just need help, he needs the Helper. Until a man gets the Helper, he is still miserable. If God is for us, no one can be against us. Thus the Bible says:

> *But as many as received him, to them*
> *gave he power to become the sons of*

God, even to them that believe on his name.

John 1:12

A son is always sure of his father's support, so a believer is always sure of God's presence, which makes him a mighty force upon the earth – one with God is a mighty host. You may not like it, but everyone that is not born again is a child of the devil. Jesus, Himself, said that in John 8:44. The Jews were mad at Him, when He addressed them in those terms. In verse 48 of the same chapter, they said: *"Say we not well that thou art a Samaritan, and hast a devil?"*

Without mincing words, however, there are two worlds: the world of darkness and the world of light. Until one is translated into the latter, he belongs to the former, where the devil is the prince. He is the chief executive; whatever he says, stands. This explains why people make hard resolutions and get nothing out of it. The new birth comes as a result of receiving the

Word of God.

> *Being born again, not of corruptible seed, but of incorruptible, by the word of God, which liveth and abideth for ever.*

1 Peter 1:23

The Word is the seed that gives rise to the new birth miracle. This means agreeing with what God says you are and what He says you can become, as you do what He says you should. It is in receiving this Word that one gets the power of salvation. In Romans 1:16, Paul says: *For I am not ashamed of the gospel of Christ: for it is the power of God unto salvation to every one that believeth; to the Jew first, and also to the Greek.* Every other blessing necessarily follows this pattern – receiving the Word and obtaining your desired result. Without the seed, there cannot be the fruit.

How can a man be born again? On the day of Pentecost, the multitude asked the same question of Peter and the disciples. They asked, *"Men and brethren, what shall we do?"* (Acts 2:37). In other words, they were asking, *"What shall we do to be saved?"* There are certain steps that the unbeliever desirous of receiving salvation must take.

First, repent. Acts 2:38 records Peter's injunction to the multitudes on the day of Pentecost: *Then Peter said unto them, Repent, and be baptized every one of you in the name of Jesus Christ for the remission of sins, and ye shall receive the gift of the Holy Ghost.*

Repentance calls for acknowledging that you are a sinner, that you are sorry for your sins, and that you are willing to forsake them. Romans 3:23 says: *For all have sinned, and come short of the glory of God.* (See also Luke 18:13; Isaiah 55:17; Luke 13:13; Acts 3:19).

Some may be deceived by their moral uprightness, and thus see no need for repentance – these may be deceived into their graves. The truth is that all have sinned and therefore, do not measure up to God's standard of righteousness. If the Bible says "all," believe that you are included. Everyone born of a woman is born a sinner, not only because of what he does, but his nature is essentially a sin nature. Through the fall of the first Adam, all have become sinners. That is why no one teaches a child to lie, and yet he knows how to cover up effectively. Therefore, your best moral standard as an unbeliever is like the filthiness of rags (Isaiah 64:6).

You need to repent. No unbeliever is acceptable to God, and if He is going to judge you at the end, is it not best to seek His justification now? It is he that God commends that is commended. The surname of every unbeliever is Sinner. This calls for your challenging it through Christ Jesus. Repent and you will be converted; your nature will undergo a dramatic change. All things will become new.

Secondly, believe that your sins are blotted out by reason of the shed Blood of Jesus Christ (Hebrews 9:22), and that God does not impute any iniquity to you any longer (Psalms 32:1). Believe in your heart that you have been given power to become a child of God (John 1:12). Believe that you are no longer that wretched sinner, but the righteousness of God in Christ Jesus (2 Corinthians 5:21). John 3:16 declares:

> *For God so loved the world, that he gave his only begotten Son, that whosoever believeth in him should not perish, but have everlasting life.*

Believe therefore, in the finished work of Christ on the cross.

Finally, confess. The Bible says:

> *For with the heart man believeth unto righteousness; and with the mouth confession is made unto salvation.*
>
> Romans 10:10

Therefore, having done what God says, you make a declaration. Confession essentially is saying the same thing with God. God says when you repent you are saved; so, you say, "I am saved." God says when you repent, your sins are forgiven; so you say, "My sins are blotted out." God says when you believe, you will not perish; so say, "I shall not perish." God says when you believe, you will have everlasting life; so say: "I have everlasting life." Say it loud: "Having taken God at His Word, I am born again"

Now, begin to desire the sincere milk of the Word that you may grow thereby (1 Pet.er 2:2). Go for it at personal and fellowship levels, and you will ever be grateful to God for your new found life.

Chapter 2

SEED TIME AND HARVEST

God made an eternal declaration in Genesis 8:22:

While the earth remaineth, seedtime and harvest, and cold and heat, and summer and winter, and day and night shall not cease.

The order is simple: from the natural point of view, there is no fruit without the seed. It is firstly the seed, and then, the harvest. If you want orange, you do not sow guavas; if you want cocoa, you do not sow cola-nut; hence the fruit you desire determines the seed you sow:

> *Be not deceived; God is not mocked: for*
> *whatsoever a man soweth, that shall he*
> *also reap.*
>
> Galatians 6:7

While explaining the parable of the sower in Luke 8:11, Jesus said the seed is the Word of God. The Word is the all-purpose seed, giving rise to salvation, healing, holiness, protection, long life, prosperity, etc. The Word is the answer to all the issues of life.

Salvation begins at the Word, for until a man gets the Word about salvation, he keeps struggling with sin. Until he gets the Word concerning divine healing, he is dominated by sickness; until a man gets the Word about divine protection, he is living at the mercy of robbers. Until you arrive at the Word of God concerning prosperity, you may die in penury. Hence, the Word is the end of all striving. The Bible declares in Matthew 7:20:

Wherefore by their fruits ye shall know them.

Thus, if one is living in divine prosperity, if you are living in divine protection, then it means you have received the Word concerning that. What happens on on the outside is determined by what is on the inside of the man. One does not argue about what one has planted in his field. He may choose to call it whatever he wants, but the fruit will show exactly what it is eventually.

For your seeds to grow, they have to be sown at the appropriate place, where the conditions for germination are met. Naturally, you do not expect your seed to grow in a refrigerator, on your dining table or to grow on your floor carpet. Just as the natural seed demands the appropriate sowing ground, so does the spiritual. In the parable of the sower, Jesus said the good ground is *"the honest and good heart"* (Luke

21

8:15). The heart is the proper place for the spiritual seed to germinate, not the head. Many people assent mentally to the Word, hence, they obtain no profit from it. One could be a university professor and an authority on the New Testament and yet be gagged by poverty, sickness, fear and defeat, because he has no spiritual grasp of the truth therein. When Adam fell, his mind was still active; he knew he needed a covering for his nakedness and also protection from wild beasts, but as we said earlier, he was already a dead man, because the real him (his spirit) was dead. The Word has to find its way into the heart of man, that real man, the spirit.

Just as a natural seed will not grow unless it is buried in the earth, so also will the spiritual seed not produce other than when it is received into the heart. The Word is knocking at your heart, not your head. Revelation 3:20 says:

22

Behold, I stand at the door, and knock: if any man hear my voice, and open the door, I will come in to him, and will sup with him, and he with me. The "I" stands for Jesus, and bless God, Jesus stands for the Word (See John 1:1-3). When you plant a seed, you expect it to bear fruit, and when you plant the Word you expect a miracle. When you plant the healing Word, you reap healing miracle. The Bible says God watches over His Words to perform them (Jeremiah 1:12). The moment the seed is planted, the husbandman will ensure that the desired result is obtained.

> *So shall my word be that goeth forth out of my mouth: it shall not return unto me void, but it shall accomplish that which I please, and it shall prosper in the thing whereto I sent it.*
>
> Isaiah 55:11

All the forces of hell can do nothing against

the Word, when it is received into the proper place. In the same way, your enemy cannot hinder the growth of your natural seed that is planted under appropriate conditions in the right place.

The Word, therefore, is not meant for the shelf; it is meant for the heart. It is not meant for the desk, but the heart. Until you come to the Word point on any issue, you should not expect any fruit. It is the seed and then the fruit. Go and get the seed and you will have the fruit. The natural seed is the source of its fruit, so also is the Word the source of all miracles. No wonder, the Bible says in 2 Timothy 2:15: *Study to shew thyself approved unto God, a workman that needeth not to be ashamed, rightly dividing the word of truth.* To study in this context means the act of seed-seeking. Thus, where one has the seed, his miracle will be approved, and he will not be afraid. Seed-seeking believers are the ever-

prosperous ones; they have got the secret. The
secret is seed before fruit.

I once ministered to a woman plagued with
barrenness. I knew that I had to get hold of the
seed in the first place. Therefore, I set myself
to search the Word of God for the appropriate
seed. After a while, I got hold of some scriptures
that stirred up faith within me. I fed these to
the woman, and she received her miracle. Bless
God, she has a child today.

Again, another Christian family had a sickler
(sickle cell anaemia) child and the case had
become very frustrating. The mother hurried
to my office on the issue. I went again into the
Word to obtain the appropriate seed for the
desired miracle. I got about eight scriptures
that forbid such in a believer's home. I became
victory-conscious, made my way to their home
and ministered to the child. The Word
produced the miracle. This child is very

Find The Appropriate Seed for Pastor Tells

healthy today.

If no man will commence praying for a big harvest of maize when in fact he has planted no seed, then, in the same way, a believer will be merely wasting his time praying for a miracle, where he has sown no seed. The question may be asked: How does one get the Word to produce? The following chapters are devoted to answering this question.

Chapter 3

PLANT BY THE RIVERS

Wise farmers should know where to plant seed. It is not merely burying the seed that matters, but burying it in the appropriate place under the appropriate conditions. Every seed requires water to grow, hence wise men plant by the rivers.

Blessed are ye that sow beside all waters, that send forth thither the feet of the ox and the ass (Isaiah 32:20). Those that plant by rivers have bountiful harvests. The river in the case of the Word of God is the Holy Ghost. John 7:37-39 records:

In the last day, that great day of the feast, Jesus stood and cried, saying, If any man thirst, let him come unto me, and drink.

He that believeth on me, as the scripture hath said, out of his belly shall flow rivers of living water.

(But this spake he of the Spirit, which they that believe on him should receive: for the Holy Ghost was not yet given; because that Jesus was not yet glorified.)

Naturally, a river makes the conditions much more favourable to the seed; so also is it spiritually. A believer filled with the Holy Spirit finds it easier to assimilate spiritual truths, much more than a believer that is not. The Bible says:

But the natural man receiveth not the things of the Spirit of God: for they are foolishness unto him...

1 Corinthians 2:14

On the other hand, one's capacity for the truth

PLANT BY THE RIVERS

increases when one is filled with the Holy
Ghost. Jesus said in John 16:12-13: *I have yet
many things to say unto you, but ye cannot
bear them now. Howbeit when he, the Spirit
of truth, is come, he will guide you into all
truth...*

This passage implies that the unbaptized
believer has no capacity to contain all truth,
even though they are valuable to him. In
another passage in John 14:26, Jesus said, the
Holy Spirit expounds the truth and brings it
to the remembrance of the believer when
called for.

Being filled with the Holy Spirit implies more
than speaking in tongues; it means being
endued with power to occupy where we belong
by covenant. The Bible says in Acts 1:8: *But ye
shall receive power, after that the Holy Ghost
is come upon you.* It is the empowering of the
Holy Spirit for spiritual efficiency.

The Holy Spirit, therefore, offers all manner of conveniences for the growth of the seed. It is the Spirit that gives life; the flesh profits nothing. Jesus said in John 6:63:

> *... the words that I speak unto you, they are spirit, and they are life.*
>
> *Without the Holy Spirit, the word remains as mere letters and*
>
> *... the letter killeth, but the spirit giveth life.*
>
> 2 Corinthians 3:6

provoca(sul)

The seed is made alive by the Spirit; without Him the seed is dead. The seed cannot produce living fruit. No wonder, many believers receive the Word and it gets easily choked up, because the Spirit to keep that Word alive is not there. It is the Spirit that makes the Word come alive; physical or intellectual ability profits nothing. Get the river of living water in you and your seed will ever be kept alive and you will surely have your harvest.

Until you understand the Word, you cannot derive any benefit from it. Remember the Ethiopian eunuch, Philip simply asked him, *"Understandest thou what thou readest?"* The eunuch replied, *"How can I, except some man should guide me?"* (Acts 8:30-31). We may well assume that the eunuch may have read this passage many times over but, for as long as he was in the dark as to what it meant, he could not profit by it. The one that puts you over today is the Holy Spirit: The Bible says, *But the manifestation of the Spirit is given to every man to profit withal* (1 Corinthians 12:7).

The Holy Spirit is referred to by Paul as *"the Spirit of wisdom and revelation"* (Ephesians 1:17). He sheds light on the Word for the believer to easily grasp it. He is the Professor of truth.

How does one receive the Holy Spirit? There is a measure of the Holy Spirit in everyone that believes on the name of the Lord Jesus Christ, but this does not mean, therefore, that all believers are thereby baptized in the Holy Spirit. Baptism in the Holy Spirit is a total different experience from salvation.

The first requirement for the baptism in the Holy Spirit is that the person making the quest must be a believer, for the baptism is sequel to salvation. In Acts 19, we are told that Paul met some disciples in Ephesus and inquired of them: *"Have ye received the Holy Ghost since ye believed?"* (Verse 2). Secondly, we have to bear in mind that the Holy Spirit has already been given, on the day of Pentecost, so we only receive Him into our hearts. Thirdly, he that seeks the Holy Spirit must create a desire in his heart for Him (Isaiah. 35:1-2). Jesus said: *If any man thirst, let him come unto Me and drink* (John 7:37). Finally, the believer has to ask. In Luke 11:13, Jesus said:

> *If ye then, being evil, know how to give good gifts unto your children: how much more shall your heavenly Father give the Holy Spirit to them that ask him?*

It has to be pointed out, of course, that the believer must necessarily speak with other tongues. There are many reasons for this. In the first place, in all cases of baptism in the Holy Spirit recorded in the Book of the Acts of the Apostles, there is a direct or indirect reference to speaking with tongues (See Acts 2:4; 10:46; 19:6).

In the case of the Samaritan believers recorded in Acts 8:17, speaking with other tongues is not mentioned directly, but there is enough indirect evidence to conclude that the recipients spoke with other tongues, too. In verse 18, we read that *When Simon saw that through laying on of the apostles' hands, the Holy*

Ghost was given, he offered them money. We can validly infer that something that could register on the senses had taken place. I think if the Samaritan believers had remained mute, it is difficult to picture what in the baptism could so appeal to Simon as to make him offer the apostles money in return for the power to lay on hands and get the same results.

The second reason is that when you speak in tongues you edify yourself (1 Corinthians 14:4). To edify means to build up spiritually. Equally important, Jude 20 says: *But ye, beloved, building up yourselves on your most holy faith, praying in the Holy Ghost.* Praying in the Holy Ghost feeds your spirit. As Paul explains in 1 Corinthians 14:14, that *"... If I pray in an unknown tongue, my spirit prayeth, but my understanding is unfruitful."* When you speak with other tongues, you are spiritually tuned to God, alone with Him (1 Corinthians 14:2).

Thirdly, the Holy Spirit helps our praying. Paul says in Romans 8:26:

> *Likewise the Spirit also helpeth our infirmities: for we know not what we should pray for as we ought: but the Spirit itself maketh intercession for us with groanings which cannot be uttered.*

When we pray in the Spirit, we assuredly pray in accordance with the will of God, so we are more certain of receiving than when we pray with the natural mind only.

Speaking in other tongues is part of the spiritual armour at our disposal and, as the spiritual battle intensifies in this end-time, we will need to bring it to bear more and more. In Ephesians 6:18, we read:

> *Praying always with all prayer and supplication in the Spirit, and watching*

thereunto with all perseverance and supplication for all saints.

It is clear that the injunction is not placed only on a section of Christians – all believers are to put on the armour of *"praying always with all prayer and supplication in the Spirit"* that is to say, "praying in tongues." Hence, talking with other tongues is not one of the nine manifestations of the Holy Ghost recorded in 1 Corinthians 12. These gifts are divided *"to every man severally as He will"* (Verse 11). If this means that talking with other tongues is a gift, which the Spirit gives to those He chooses, then the Spirit would have left some believers without one of the spiritual armours! But God be blessed, not everyone can prophesy, yet everyone can talk with other tongues and thus pray in the Holy Ghost. Neither need the believer be confused by 1 Corinthians 12:30, where Paul asks, *"Do all speak with tongues?"*

Here the apostle is essentially speaking of the gift of diversities of tongues (Verse 28) which is reserved for select believers, just as, the gift of the working of miracles, is the preserve of only some believers.

Do not rob yourself of a weapon that is going to be one of the decisive means of waging the war of the age. Be baptized in the Holy Ghost.

Chapter 4

BELIEVE THE WORD

The Word is of no effect, until faith is mixed with it. The Bible says in Hebrews 4:2:

> *For unto us was the gospel preached, as well as unto them: but the word preached did not profit them, not being mixed with faith in them that heard it.*

This is saying in effect that, profit can only be derived from the Word of faith. It is not to you according to your knowledge, it is to you according to your faith. The Prophet Isaiah wrote, *"...If ye will not believe, surely ye shall not be established"* (Isaiah 7:9). The Word is not established until it is believed. It is faith that draws virtue from the Word, as it happened in the case of the woman with the issue of blood. If you touch the Word of God right now with your faith, the virtue in that Word will flow into your body.

As an illustration, a farmer who does not believe in the natural process of germination may keep removing his seed to determine its progress. His action reveals his unbelief, which destroys the seed. When a believer is not believing the Word, he is like this farmer, and he is not likely to get his desired result. Naturally, the seed is meant to remain buried in the earth for a time and then it will shoot up. Thus, the farmer who believes and leaves his seed in the earth will surely have his harvest. In the same way, a believer who sticks to the Word by faith cannot but have his miracle. The Bible says in Luke 1:45:

And blessed is she that believed: for there

shall be a performance of those things which were told her from the Lord.

The reason is that God will forever back up His Word. So, whenever a man stands on the Word, God is always prepared to bring it to pass. God, says the Bible, watches over His Word to perform it (See Isaiah 55:11; Jeremiah 1;12). God knows when you are believing and when you are not. Faith is an operation of the inside, God sees in secret and rewards openly (Matthew 6:18). All men may commend your faith, but it is he that God commends that is commended. The Lord said to Samuel:

... Look not on his countenance, or on the height of his stature; because I have refused him: for the LORD seeth not as man seeth; for man looketh on the outward appearance, but the LORD looketh on the heart.

1 Samuel 16:7

41

At Lystra, Paul perceived that the impotent man had faith to be healed, and so ordered him to stand on his feet and walk (Acts 14:9-10). In another episode in Mark 2:3-5, Jesus saw a paralytic man being brought down through the roof. In verse 5, the Bible says Jesus *"saw their faith."* Their faith had translated into action, and they had the miracle they desired. Until faith has arisen in your heart, your miracle is not at hand.

Until your Faith is in your Heart And God sees it, your miracle will Not manifest

Chapter 5

DO THE WORD

To every miracle there is a man-ward side. God requires something from the one that *word* desires a miracle, and if any man will heed God's requirements, he certainly will have his miracle. At Cana of Galilee, the wine got exhausted before the end of the wedding feast. People desired a miracle. Mary, the mother of Jesus, under the unction of the Holy Spirit gave them a major key into the miraculous. Said she:

Whatsoever He saith unto you, do it.

John 2:5

Mary was saying, in effect, that for a miracle to be, they had to do anything He told them to do, whether or not it appealed to them. Doing whatever Jesus said, was the only way to having their miracle.

It may appear foolish, but know that *"the foolishness of God is wiser than men"* (1 Corinthians 1:25). Whatever God tells you to do, do it. God cannot be Lord of your situation, when you are not ready to do what He tells you to do. In the case under consideration, the people were desperately in need of wine, but Jesus asked them to fill water pots with water. That looked funny, but it was the only truth that would bring the answer. The pots were in the open; they could be seen pouring water into them and certainly, some may even have laughed them to scorn. That, however, was the only way to get the answer.

"Whatsoever He saith unto you, do it." The ones mocking you will soon begin to shout, "Hosanna", upon the arrival of your miracle.

Jesus said in Luke 9:26:

> *For whosoever shall be ashamed of me*
> *and of my words, of him shall the Son*
> *of man be ashamed, when he shall come*
> *in his own glory...*

If you do not want secret blessings, then be ready for public obedience. Despise the shame and press on for your miracle. To have the miracle of salvation, you must not be too ashamed to repent. To receive from above, you have to do the asking. To be free, you have to know. If you feel too wise to give, then you cannot have divine intervention in your financial situation. If you are too busy to pray, then you should not expect to receive. In every miracle that comes your way, you have a part to play.

2 Kings 5:9-12 tells the story of Naaman, the captain of the Syrian army. Naaman considered the prophet's instruction to wash himself in the

Jordan too demeaning, and thereby came close to missing his miracle. Obedience brings possession. When he was later persuaded by his servants and obeyed the word of the prophet, he had his miracle.

Yes

> *Then went he down, and dipped himself seven times in Jordan, according to the saying of the man of God: and his flesh came again like unto the flesh of a little child, and he was clean.*
>
> (2 Kings 5:14)

wow !!!.

Obedience is the key factor to walking in the realm of the miraculous. Whether what the Word says applies to reason or not, go ahead and do it.

There was a widow in Zarephath in the days of the prophet Elijah. A demand that appeared curious was made of the woman by the prophet. It was a hard time in Israel then; a relentless famine was ravaging the land, and here came

Elijah asking this widow for a morsel of bread. It was a pathetic response indeed that the widow gave him. She said, *"As the Lord thy God liveth, I have not a cake, but an handful of meal in a barrel, and a little oil in a cruse; and behold, I am gathering two sticks, that I may go in and dress it for me and my son, that we may eat and die* (1 Kings 17:!2). It must have been a very horrible situation indeed. People were going consciously to their graves. But this "wicked" prophet would not give up. He said to her: *"Fear not, go and do as thou hast said: but make me thereof a little cake first, and bring it unto me, and after make for thee and for thy son."* The woman may well have asked in her surprise, "You mean I should make for you a cake first?"

Bless God the widow went ahead and did according to the word of the man of God. *And the barrel of meal wasted not, neither did the cruse of oil fail, according to the word of the LORD, which he spake by Elijah* (1 Kings 17:16).

good

The widow paved her way through obedience into the miraculous. You could do that too. His *"Commandments are not grievous"* (1 John 5:3b). Anything He demands of you is principally for your benefit. God does not need to be saved, He Himself is the Saviour. When He tells you to repent, it is so that you will escape eternal damnation. God does not need to be free; Himself sets man free. When, therefore, He asks you to come and learn of His Word, it is for your benefit. He declares in Matthew 11:28-29: *Come unto me, all ye that labour and are heavy laden, and I will give you rest. Take my yoke upon you, and learn of me; for I am meek and lowly in heart: and ye shall find rest unto your souls.*

God does not need prosperity, for all the silver

and gold are His (Haggai 2:8). So, when He asks you to give, it is in order for you to prosper financially. The Bible says in Isaiah 1:19:

> *If ye be willing and obedient, ye shall eat the good of the land*

God demands willing obedience from you, not doing it grudgingly, but from your willing heart. Whenever God pronounces blessings for His people, He leaves a part for them to do.

> *This book of the law shall not depart out of thy mouth; but thou shalt meditate therein day and night, that thou mayest observe to do according to all that is written therein: for then thou shalt make thy way prosperous, and then thou shalt have good success.*

> Joshua 1:8

Prosperity and good success come not just as a result of confessing the Word, but DOING

IT. Deuteronomy 28:1-2 dwells on the rewards of doing the Word too:

> *And it shall come to pass, if thou shalt hearken diligently unto the voice of the LORD thy God, to observe and to do all his commandments which I command thee this day, that the LORD thy God will set thee on high above all nations of the earth:*
>
> *And all these blessings shall come on thee, and overtake thee, if thou shalt hearken unto the voice of the LORD thy God.*

A man will get nowhere, until he is ready to do what God says. You may pray and fast and get nothing, if you are walking in outright disobedience to the Word of God. God has more respect for His Word than He has for His name (Ps. 138:2). Faith in the Word cannot get for you the blessings of the word whose demands you have not met. That is why: Jesus, in Luke

12:47 says *"And that servant, which knew his lord's will, and prepared not himself, neither did according to his will, shall be beaten with many stripes."*

As a believer, therefore, know that walking in wilful disobedience leads you into suffering. Many believers are financially oppressed because they know the will of God, but refuse to do it, so God Himself is putting a hole in their pockets (Haggai 1:6).

It is immensely profitable to heed the Word and haste to do it, for to obey is better than sacrifice (1 Samuel 15:22).

Chapter 6

FOCUS ON THE WORD

There is power in looking. The miracle power of the Word can be released through looking. It is recorded in Numbers 21 Chapter that when the Israelites spoke against God and Moses, the Lord sent fiery serpents among them and many died. However, because God is full of mercy and compassion, He designed a way out for them when they repented:

Therefore the people came to Moses, and said, We have sinned, for we have spoken against the LORD, and against thee; pray unto the LORD, that he take away the serpents from us. And Moses prayed for the people.

And the LORD said unto Moses, Make

> *thee a fiery serpent, and set it upon a*
> *pole: and it shall come to pass, that every*
> *one that is bitten, when he looketh upon*
> *it, shall live.*
>
> Numbers 21:7-8.

God was showing an eternal pattern with respect to the miraculous, in this episode. Everyone that looked, lived. Bless God, that was only a shadow of the real thing, for in John 3:14, Jesus said, *And as Moses lifted up the serpent in the wilderness, even so must the Son of man be lifted up.* Jesus is seen here as playing the role of that brazen serpent. Jesus is the Word of God (John 1:1-2; 5:7; 19:13).

If we will look at the Word today as they looked at the serpent in the wilderness, we will without doubt derive a miraculous virtue from it. The Bible declares in Psalms 34:5, ***They looked unto him, and were lightened: and their faces were not ashamed.*** Everyone that looks will receive light, and scripturally, light is synonymous with life. You derive miraculous life from looking at the Word.

As Jesus said in Matthew 6:22: *The light of the body is the eye: if therefore thine eye be single, thy whole body shall be full of light.* Let the Word have all your attention. Do not give in to any distraction. Do not allow the pains in your body to draw your attention from the fact that by the stripes of Jesus you were healed. Let your "eye be single," focused solely on the Word, and your body will be full of the miraculous – the life of God. There is power in looking.

> *My son, attend to my words; incline thine ear unto my sayings.*
>
> *Let them not depart from thine eyes; keep them in the midst of thine heart.*
>
> *For they are life unto those that find them, and health to all their flesh.*
>
> Proverbs 4:20-22

The emphasis here is again on looking: "let them not depart from your EYES." Keep looking at the Word; it shall be life to you and health to all your flesh. There is a miracle power in looking at the Word.

The Holy Ghost spoke to me one day from 2 Corinthians 3:18,

> *But we all, with open face beholding as in a glass the glory of the Lord, are changed into the same image from glory to glory, even as by the Spirit of the Lord.*

It was revealed to me that the glass mentioned here refers to the Word of God. James 1:23-25 makes this abundantly clear. I began to see that if a man will keep an open face at the scriptures, he will continue to be transformed from glory to glory. That must be the miraculous.

The believer today has to spend time looking

at the Word. Are you suffering in any particular area of your life? Go to the Word with an *"open face"*, and you will draw divine virtue from it. The Psalmist says in Psalm 121:1: ***I will lift up mine eyes unto the hills, from whence cometh my help.*** From the beginning of this book, we have said over and again that your help is in the Word of God; so focus your eyes there, and your help will come.

YES SO TRUE

Are you facing the problem of unemployment? You have read some scriptures concerning that, you have heard preachers quote some, and you have no doubt been prayed for to get a job. Maybe, you need to settle down, bring out those scriptures and fix your eyes on them, and you will soon see the miracle power of God at work. There is power in looking.

Tell This to TELLS BOLTON

Chapter 7

STORE UP THE WORD

You draw virtue in time of need from the Word stored up in your heart. Most of the battles of life come all of a sudden, and whether you stand or fall has to do with how much substance is in you. Jesus said to Simon Peter,

> *... Simon, Simon, behold, Satan hath desired to have you, that he may sift you as wheat:*
>
> *But I have prayed for thee, that thy faith fail not: and when thou art converted, strengthen thy brethren.*
>
> Luke 22:31-32

The devil is busy sifting men, but he can only

succeed with feather-weight believers. Fill your heart with the correct stuff, that is, the Word of God, or errors will fill your heart. Jesus pointed out in Matthew 12:43-45 that the evil spirit that has been cast out of his place of abode, prowls to and fro, and will always check back to see if anything else has taken up his place. When he discovers the place neat but empty, he not only comes back, but he also invites others along. Too many believers today are neat but empty; they cannot continue to be neat for long without substance in their hearts.

The Bible says the devil is the *"prince of the power of the air"* (Ephesians 2:2). Wherever there is air, the devil has room in which to operate. If you must be free, then you must store up the correct stuff in the heart.

If thou faint in the day of adversity, thy strength is small (Proverbs 24:10). Less than enough strength cannot sustain anyone in the day of battle. If you must continue in the race, you must take food. As the angel told Elijah in 1 Kings 19:7: *Arise and eat; because the journey is too great for thee.* **Elijah** *went in the strength of that meat forty days and forty nights* (Verse 8).

The stored Word is the only resistance against the devil and his works. It is easy for the devil to prevail, if you have no rich store of the Word.

> *Let the word of Christ dwell in you richly in all wisdom...*
>
> Colossians 3:16

Paul is exhorting you here to get a rich store of the Word. Every temptation comes as a wave in the mind, and if the mind is not being adequately renewed by the Word of God, the individual in question falls flat. Stealing, adultery, fornication, cheating, lying, anger, envy, etc, all gain access through the mind.

However, you can keep your mind in constant spiritual gear by the Word. The Psalmist said in Psalms 119:11: *Thy word have I hid in mine heart, that I might not sin against thee.* With the Word inside you, sin has no place in you. The Spirit spoke through John the Apostle on the same theme: *Whosoever is born of God doth not commit sin; for his seed remaineth in him: and he cannot sin, because he is born of God* (1 John 3:9). *"CANNOT SIN."* That is exciting! This is because darkness and light cannot co-exist. *"Light shineth in darkness, and the darkness comprehended it not,"* said John in John 1:5. Put in the Word and you will get rid of sin. Keep replenishing your "Word Bank" and you will soon discover how easy it is to keep your body under and overcome the forces of evil.

Be a Word addict and you will stop struggling with the devil and all his forces.

"Keep (the word) in the midst of thine heart," admonishes Proverbs 4:21. Having done so, you will get life and health to all your flesh. Every Word stored up in your heart is a miracle seed: in due season you will have your harvest. *yes*

You never can have enough. In 1 Corinthians 8:2, Paul wrote: *And if any man think that he knoweth any thing, he knoweth nothing yet as he ought to know.* There is more to learn, *yes* and more to discern. No one can ever get it all. *"His ways are past finding out"* (Romans 11:33).

No one starts looking for weapons to use in the heat of battle; every soldier goes to war battle-ready. In 2 Timothy 2:15, Paul cautions Timothy to *"Study to shew thyself approved unto God, a workman that needeth not to be ashamed, rightly dividing the word of truth."* Paul was instructing the young soldier, Timothy, to acquire knowledge of the Word, so that he could be pronounced (approved) battle-ready, as one correctly able to apply the Word (weapon of warfare) and thereby not be ashamed in the heat of battle. Get your weapons and begin to prove them, and you will be skilful at handling such when war strikes. You need to settle down with the Word. Jesus said in Matthew 12:35:

> *A good man out of the good treasure of the heart bringeth forth good things: and an evil man out of the evil treasure bringeth forth evil things.*

Get a good Word bank and you will always have enough from which to draw your miracles.

PREACH THIS

Chapter 8

TALK THE WORD

What you believe only becomes effective when it is spoken. It is with the heart you believe, but you do the confession with the mouth. Faith comes by hearing with the ear and goes forth for operation by speaking with the mouth. Jesus said in Mark 11:23:

> *For verily I say unto you, That whosoever shall say unto this mountain, Be thou removed, and be thou cast into the sea; and shall not doubt in his heart, but shall believe that those things which he saith shall come to pass; he shall have whatsoever he saith.*

You have what you say. A believer whose

mouth is always shut has a lot to lose. Your mouth is one of your spiritual weapons.

> *For I will give you a mouth and wisdom, which all your adversaries shall not be able to gainsay nor resist.*
>
> Luke 21:15

Say it loud; shout it on the housetop. There is a creative force behind the words of your mouth. When you begin to make Biblical declarations, you are talking yourself into the realm of the supernatural. Your mouth is not given to you just for food and drink, but also as an outlet for creative words, like Abraham calling *"those things that be not as though they were."*

When all those around are talking fear, you are talking security because of the Word you have inside you. When all around you are talking failure, you are talking good success on the basis of the Word. All talk lack and want, and you keep talking prosperity. Jesus said:

> *Whosoever therefore shall be ashamed of me and of my words in this adulterous and sinful generation; of him also shall the Son of man be ashamed, when he cometh in the glory of his Father with the holy angels.*
>
> Mark 8:38

You are a peculiar person. Confess the Word boldly before men. God also will become proud of you on His throne. Declare it boldly. The God, who delivered Daniel out of the den of lions, is still alive today. Shout it out; the one that rendered the burning fiery furnace ineffective is still on His throne, and in the same way that He delivered the three Hebrew boys, so will He deliver you.

A lady was on her death bed, about to breathe her last breath, but who with all her remaining strength kept saying, *"I shall not die but live, and declare the works of the Lord"* (Psalms 118:17). Praise God, she is alive today. Talk your life into the miraculous. The Bible declares in Proverbs 18:21 that,

> *Death and life are in the power of the tongue: and they that love it shall eat the fruit thereof.*

Poverty and prosperity, health and sickness, fear and security, all lie in the tongue. If you talk health, you will be healthy; if you talk sickness, you will be sick. Talk prosperity and you will be prosperous – what you say is what you will have. God gave Joshua this charge in Joshua 1:8,

> *This book of the law shall not depart out of thy mouth; but thou shalt meditate therein day and night, that thou mayest observe to do according to*

all that is written therein: for then thou
shalt make thy way prosperous, and
then thou shalt have good success.

God is saying here, in effect, that you should
let others say what they may, you keep talking
the Word. The wisdom in this was proved at
Kadesh Barnea. 10 of the 12 spies sent by Moses
to spy out the land of Canaan swore to the
impossibility of taking the land; but Joshua
stood up with Caleb and said, *"We are well able*
to overcome it" (See Numbers 13:25-30; 14:6-
10). Joshua and Caleb remembered the Word
concerning the land of Canaan and declared it.
The majority has no relevance to victory in
spiritual battles: the one with the Word will
always overcome, even if he is just one in a
million.

Stop talking what the majority of people are
talking today; start talking *"thus saith the Lord"*
and you will ever triumph. Joshua and Caleb

stood on the Word, declared it and they overcame. Paul told the Corinthians:

> *We having the same spirit of faith, according as it is written, I believed, and therefore have I spoken; we also believe, and therefore speak*
>
> 2 Corinthians 4:13

Believing and speaking is the spirit of faith. God is a faith God, but He is also a speaking God.

"And God said..." (Genesis 1:3). His faith became creative at His Word. In Romans 10:10, we read: ***For with the heart man believeth unto righteousness; and with the mouth confession is made unto salvation.*** You do not get the effect of what you believe in your heart, without saying it with your mouth.

Confession is made unto, not just salvation from sin, but also from poverty and sickness.

70

Keep speaking the Word and your mountain will become a plain. Say what God says about your work, your health, your home, your finance, etc, and you will have them. The Bible says:

> *How forcible are right words!*
>
> Job 6:25

Your words will either make or break you. Get your deliverance from idle words, for the Bible says you will pay for them (Matthew 12:36). Pray with David the Psalmist, *Set a watch, O LORD, before my mouth; keep the door of my lips* (Psalms 141:3).

Chapter 9

MEDITATE ON THE WORD

This is a forgotten art of the Church, yet it is one of the most important keys to successful Christian living. There is power in meditation. Men who have won any notable battles in the on-going spiritual war, have meditation as one of their principal weapons of warfare.

Meditation can be said to be a spiritual means by which the Word of God is imparted to the natural process of absorption of the physical food that we take. Food becomes valuable only when it is absorbed into the blood stream, where it adds to the physical build-up of the individual concerned. God gave Joshua the following charge:

> *This book of the law shall not depart*
> *out of thy mouth; but thou shalt meditate*
> *therein day and night, that thou mayest*
> *observe to do according to all that is*
> *written therein: for then thou shalt make*
> *thy way prosperous, and then thou shalt*
> *have good success.*
>
> Joshua 1:8

God, Himself, recommends meditation. Prosperity, spiritually has to do with meditation. Physical, material and financial prosperity come only as a result of spiritual prosperity. John the Apostle wrote in 3 John 2: ***Beloved, I wish above*** ***all things that thou mayest prosper and be in*** ***health, even as thy soul prospereth***. The reason you have not arrived at that level of prosperity you are believing God for, is that your spirit is not capable of containing it.

Shortly before the crucifixion, Jesus told His

disciples that He had many things to tell them, but that they could not bear them then (John 16:12). Hence, even though those things would be valuable to them, they had to be ripe for them before they could be told. Many of us are believing God for certain things, but God does not see us as yet adequately equipped for them. He said, *"I have yet many things to say unto you but ye cannot bear them now."*

If we must have the prosperity we so earnestly desire, meditation is one of the means open to us to have such established to us.

From the passage quoted from the Book of Joshua, God was saying in effect, "Joshua, as you meditate on my Word, you will be able to know which applies where, and when, and you will then be in a position to do whatever my Word commands." Meditation, in sum, helps the believer to be vigilant. He learns to be alert enough to know when God is at work and when the devil is prowling. Meditation also equips us with the power to see whatever God commands as possible and to go ahead to do it.

The Holy Spirit renders the importance of this great art in another form in Psalms 1:2-3:

> *But his delight is in the law of the Lord;*
> *and in his law doth he meditate day and night.*
>
> *And he shall be like a tree planted by the rivers*
> *of water, that bringeth forth his fruit in his*
> *season; his leaf also shall not wither, and*
> *whatsoever he doeth shall prosper.*

Meditation makes a believer fruitful and flourishing. There is miracle power in meditation.

I fell to pondering on the man Daniel of the scriptures one day, during a taxi ride in the middle of an examination period in college. One thing struck me then: it was the fact that Daniel and his three Hebrew classmates were

10 times better than their Babylonian colleagues. The Holy Spirit began to expound the matter in my heart. I said to myself: if people who lived in the days of the devil's reign made it that much, how much more should I make it now that the devil has been overthrown by the Lord Jesus Christ! If people that lived under the ministration of death were that much successful, how much more should a man be, under this *"better covenant based on better promises."* If in the days when men had no promise of "soundness of mind" they had made it that much, how much more should a New Testament believer make it today in the area of skill and learning!

There is power in Biblical meditation. As I carefully pondered these facts, a spiritual operation began to take place in my heart; there was a renewal taking place, my understanding began to sharpen up. It was in this attitude I began to prepare for one of my papers. A shower dawned on me, until I found myself commenting, "It is too much," not merely for the sake of confessing, but in absolute truth and in deed. I wrote the examination in this mood and for the first time ever, I scored hundred per cent in a mathematics paper! There is power in meditation.

Meditation is a means by which a believer brings himself to a spiritual plane, from where he can apply the force of scripture to particular everyday realities. One arrives at a point of faith easily through meditation. The believer is not called upon to meditate on problems, but on scriptures (Luke 21:14).

Your ability to diagnose your problem is not called for in spiritual warfare; but your ability to accurately divide scriptures in battle is certainly a prerequisite for this is what gets you on top. Paul told the Phillipians,

Finally, brethren, whatsoever things are true, whatsoever things are honest, whatsoever things are just, whatsoever things are pure, whatsoever things are lovely, whatsoever things are of good report; if there be any virtue, and if there be any praise, think on these things.

Philllipians 4:8

This is giving guidelines on the art of meditation – those things that should exercise your mind during your meditation hour. *"Good report"* here means faith. Evil report, as was delivered by the 10 co-spies of Joshua and Caleb, means unbelief. The elders, according to Hebrews 11, had obtained a good report, and the chapter proceeds to catalogue the exploits they achieved through faith. Think faith thoughts. Think in line with scriptures. Proverbs 23:7 says, *"As a man thinks in his heart, so is he."* Your thought life matters a lot in whether you succeed or fail in life. Your thoughts either break or make you. This is why you should renew your mind adequately with scriptures, so that your thought life can be scripturally disciplined.

"How can I develop a quality meditation life?", you may ask.

In the first place, increase your Word bank. Set yourself to store up adequate amounts of Scripture in your heart. Secondly, mind what company you keep. Psalms 1 says: *Blessed is the man that walketh not in the counsel of the ungodly, nor standeth in the way of sinners, nor sitteth in the seat of the scornful.* See also Proverbs 13:20). Thirdly, study to be quiet. The art of meditation calls for quietness. Finally, a solitary place offers a richer opportunity for quality meditation. A good example is recorded in Genesis 24:63,

> *And Isaac went out to meditate in the field at the eventide*

There is miracle power in meditation.

Chapter 10

PRAY THE WORD

The Word of God becomes fire, when released in prayer. A word-praying believer is ever an overcomer. Word-praying is right praying. James the Apostle wrote:

> *Ye ask, and receive not, because ye ask amiss, that ye may consume it upon your lusts.*
>
> James 4:3

There is a wrong way of asking and a right way of asking. Some "praying giants" have never got on the line with God. They are "storming" the heavens, they claim, but it is doubtful whether the heavens have ever so much as registered the slightest of tremors from their direction.

God does answer prayers, but one has to get on the line with Him. The Bible way of getting through is to get on the Word-line. In 1 John 5:14-15, we read,

So goas (handwritten margin note)

> **And this is the confidence that we have in him, that, if we ask any thing according to his will, he heareth us:**

> **And if we know that he hear us, whatsoever we ask, we know that we have the petitions that we desired of him.**

"His will is His WORD" (handwritten margin note)

The Apostle John is here saying, in effect, that you are not heard in heaven until you are praying according to His will. That is certainly exciting news. What is His will? It is His Word!

A man leaves a will behind for his beneficiaries in words or in writing. The will of the testator can only be known through the words he left behind. God's will is the package of the Holy Bible. God's will is as contained in the Book of Genesis through the Book of Revelation. A testator has no other will, apart from what he has left behind in words. God has no other will, apart from what He has bequeathed into us in the Holy Written Word. The Word of God is His correct phone number. If you desire to have audience with God in prayers, get through with the Word in your heart.

Any time you want your line to go through, you must dial the Word. The Book of the Acts of the Apostles records a spectacular breakthrough of the apostles to the throne, during one of their prayer sessions.

> *And when they heard that, they lifted up their voice to God with one accord, and said, Lord, thou art God, which hast made heaven, and earth, and the sea, and all that in them is:*

Who by the mouth of thy servant David hast said, Why did the heathen rage, and the people imagine vain things?

The kings of the earth stood up, and the rulers were gathered together against the Lord, and against his Christ.

For of a truth against thy holy child Jesus, whom thou hast anointed, both Herod, and Pontius Pilate, with the Gentiles, and the people of Israel, were gathered together,

For to do whatsoever thy hand and thy counsel determined before to be done.

And now, Lord, behold their threatenings: and grant unto thy servants, that with all boldness they may speak thy word,

By stretching forth thine hand to heal; and that signs and wonders may be done by the name of thy holy child Jesus.

And when they had prayed, the place was shaken where they were assembled together; and they were all filled with the Holy Ghost, and they spake the word of God with boldness.

Acts 4:24-31

This is how to get through to the throne; this is how to "storm" the heavens with prayers! This is how to pray the Word. This is how to dial the throne.

The apostles got through to the throne with praise and worship contained in verse 24, and dialed Him directly through a prophecy of David, the patriarch, in verse 25, following. Then God Himself picked up the phone at the other end, and the discussion took off.

There is no other way to do it. Jesus said, *I am the door of the sheep* (John 10:7). In John 14:6, He stated that *"no one cometh unto the Father, but by Me."* In 1 Timothy 2:5, Paul

85

wrote: *For there is one God, and one mediator between God and men, the man Christ Jesus.* The Bible makes it clear that Jesus Christ is the Word of God personified: *In the beginning was the Word, and the Word was with God, and the Word was God. The same was in the beginning with God.* (John 1:1-2). Again in 1 John 5:8, we read, *And there are three that bear witness in earth, the Spirit, and the water, and the blood: and these three agree in one.*

All of these scriptures point to the fact that you cannot get through to God outside His Word. Your prayer receives the attention of the throne, only when it is with the Word.

If anything must come to you from above, it has to be by asking. Jesus says in Matthew 7:8, that everyone that asks receives. It is not he that knows, neither he that believes, nor he that confesses, but he that asks. This is the fundamental law in receiving from God. Just as your cheque must be presented at the counter before it is cashed, so also must your prayer be on record before the request contained therein can be granted.

> *"...Ye have not, because YE ASK NOT"*
> James 4:2

Word-praying is miracle-praying. Out of the ordinary things come the way of praying. The time of the *"latter rain"* is here; the time to get the showers to come down is now. The prayer weapon is today required as never before. If we must have the showers, we must pray. It is written in Zechariah 10:1,

> **Ask ye of the LORD rain in the time of the latter rain; so the LORD shall make bright clouds, and give them showers of rain, to every one grass in the field.**

God has promised a greater out-pouring of

His power over this generation. We must get on the prayer-line until we see it established. Get on the line with God in prayers.

Word-praying changes things!

Word-praying will always produce!

Get on the line with the Word and secure your miracle. Halleluyah!

ABOUT THE *Author*

Dr. David Oyedepo is the President and Founder of Living Faith Church Worldwide a.k.a. Winners' Chapel International, with a network of churches across all cities, towns and most villages of Nigeria and over 60 other nations that spread across five major continents of the world. His faith-based teachings have literally transformed millions of lives.

To date, he has published over 60 highly impactful titles covering a range of issues, with over seven million copies in circulation.

He is the Senior Pastor of the 50,000 - seat church sanctuary - Faith Tabernacle, Canaan Land, Ota, a suburb of Lagos, Nigeria reputed to be the largest church auditorium in the world, where presently four services run every Sunday morning.

As an educationist, his mission is currently leading a revolution in education in Nigeria, with the establishment of educational institutions at all levels - primary, secondary and tertiary including the renowned Covenant University and the newly established Landmark University, where he serves as Chancellor. His educational movement is fast spreading to other African nations.

He is married to Faith and they are blessed with sons and daughters.

Books By Dr. David Oyedepo

- The Unlimited Power Of Faith
- In Pursuit Of Vision
- Pillars Of Destiny
- Signs & Wonders Today
- Exploits In Ministry
- Winning The War Against Poverty
- Walking In Dominion
- Possessing Your Possession
- The Wisdom That Works
- Exploits Of Faith
- Anointing For Exploits
- Understanding The Power Of Praise
- Walking In Newness Of Life
- Maximise Destiny
- Commanding The Supernatural
- Winning Invisible Battles
- Success Systems
- Understanding Financial Prosperity
- Success Strategies
- Understanding Your Covenant Right
- Miracle Meal
- Exploring the Riches of Redemption
- Anointing For Breakthrough
- Excellency Of Wisdom
- Breaking Financial Hardship
- The Release Of Power
- Walking In The Miraculous
- Satan Get Lost!

INSIDE VIEW OF
Faith Tabernacle

OUTSIDE VIEW OF FAITH TABERNACLE

CHURCH MASS TRANSIT— Over 250 buses commuting the worshippers to Church from all nook and crannies of Lagos & environs

Dr. David Oyedepo is the founding president of the Living Faith Church Worldwide Inc. And senior pastor of the Faith Tabernacle, a 50,000 capacity sanctuary located in Canaan Land, Ota, a suburb of Lagos Nigeria.

The construction of this gigantic architectural masterpiece was completed within twelve months and dedicated on September 18, 1999. Built totally debt free and without any foreign inputs! To God alone be all the glory.

Today, Faith Tabernacle stands as the home of signs and wonders for men and women all over the world who keep coming in droves to worship the King of kings and Lord of lords, Jesus Christ the Son of the Living God.

Visit our website for more information: www.davidoyedepoministries.org

Aerial View Of Covenant University

College of Business & Social Sciences

Covenant University

D r. David Oyedepo is the visioner and Chancellor of Covenant University founded 21st October 2002. Today, Covenant University has student population of over 6,000, all fully boarded on campus; in a state of the art halls of residence. All degree programmes offered at Covenant University are fully accredited by the appropriate accrediting body. As at date, CU offers 42 degree programmes in 3 different faculties:

COLLEGE OF SCIENCE AND TECHNOLOGY:

Computer Science, Management Information System, Architecture, Building Technology, Estate Management, Industrial Mathematics, Industrial Chemistry, Industrial Physics, Biochemistry, Biology, Microbiology, Computer Engineering, Information and Communication Technology, Electrical and Electronic Engineering, Civil Engineering, Mechanical Engineering, Chemical Engineering, Petroleum Engineering.

COLLEGE OF HUMAN DEVELOPMENT:

Philosophy, Psychology, Counseling, English Language, Mass Communication, Public Relations and Advertising, Sociology and French.

COLLEGE OF BUSINESS AND SOCIAL SCIENCES:

Accounting, Taxation and Public Sector Accounting, Banking and Finance, Business Administration, Marketing, Industrial Relations and Human Resource Management, Economics, Demography and Social Statistics, International Relations, Political Science, Public Administration, Policy and Strategic Studies.

More Facilities@ Covenant University

College of Science & Technology

University Library (Centre For Learning Resources)

4,000 Seat Students Chapel

More Facilities@ Covenant University

Post Graduate Building

Senior Staff Residential Quarters

Covenant University 100 Room Ultra Modern Guest House

Students Hall Of Residence

Landmark University

Senate Building

Landmark University is a product of the education mandate given to Dr. David Oyedepo. Dedicated on the 21st of March 2011, it is the second university to be established by his ministry.

The vision of the university is to raise leaders with particular emphasis of promoting agricultural enterprise among others with a learning focus that makes a graduate bread winners, job creators and solution providers

The teaching, research and community service of the university are weaved around the intellectual and natural resource endowment of her immediate community.

Landmark University Offer the following courses:

COLLEGE OF AGRICULTURAL SCIENCES:
General Agriculture, Animal Science, Plant Science, Agricultural Extension & Rural Development, Agricultural Economics.

COLLEGE OF SCIENCE & ENGINEERING:
Industrial Chemistry, Industrial Mathematics, Industrial Physics, Computer Science, Biology, Biochemistry, Microbiology, Electrical And Information Engineering, Mechanical Engineering, Chemical Engineering, Civil Engineering, Agricultural Engineering.

COLLEGE OF BUSINESS & SOCIAL SCIENCES:
Accounting, Banking And Finance, Business Administration, Economics, Sociology, Political Science, International Relations.

Visit our website for more information: **www.landmarkuniversity.edu.ng**

More Facilities@ Landmark University

University Chapel

College Building

Cafetaria

More Facilities@ Landmark University

One of the Student's Halls Of Residence

Professors Village

Staff Quarters